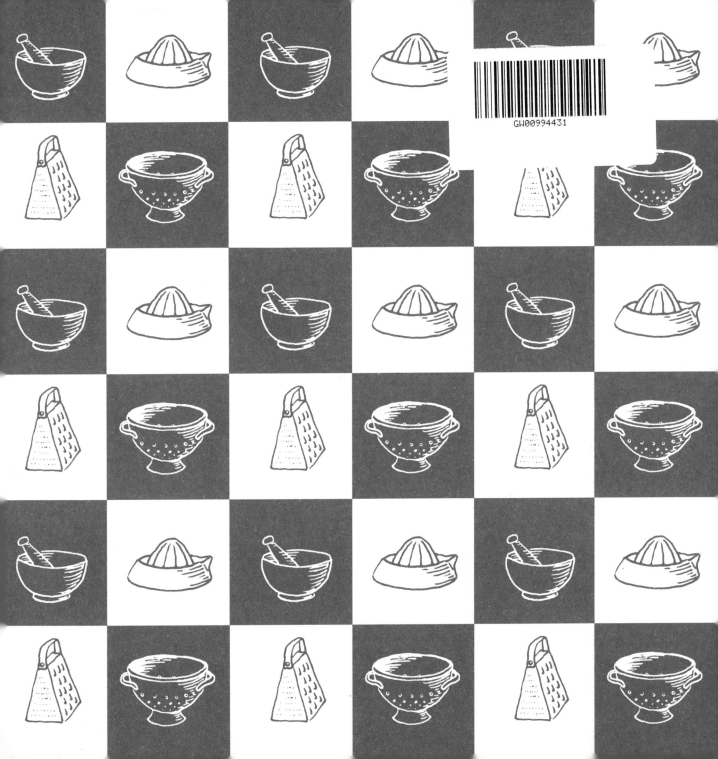

B A S I L

BASIL

A Book of Recipes

INTRODUCTION BY KATE WHITEMAN

LORENZ BOOKS

First published by Lorenz Books
an imprint of
Anness Publishing Limited
Hermes House
88-89 Blackfriars Road
London SE1 8HA

This edition distributed in Canada by Raincoast Books
8680 Cambie Street, Vancouver, British Columbia V6P 6M9

ISBN 1-85967-364-3

A CIP catalogue record is available from the British Library

Publisher Joanna Lorenz
Senior Cookery Editor Linda Fraser
Project Editor Anne Hildyard
Designer Bill Mason
Illustrations Anna Koska

Photographers Karl Adamson, Edward Allwright, Steve Baxter, James Duncan,
John Freeman, Michelle Garrett, Amanda Heywood, Patrick McLeavey,
Michael Michaels and Thomas Odulate
Recipes Kit Chan, Jacqueline Clark, Maxine Clark, Roz Denny, Nicola Diggins, Joanna Farrow,
Christine France, Sarah Gates, Shirley Gill, Patricia Lousada, Annie Nichols,
Liz Trigg, Laura Washburn and Steven Wheeler
Food for photography Carla Capalbo, Elizabeth Wolf-Cohen, Wendy Lee,
Jenny Shapter and Jane Stevenson
Stylists Madeleine Brehaut, Hilary Guy, Blake Minton and Kirsty Rawlings
Jacket photography Janine Hosegood

For all recipes, quantities are given in both metric and imperial measures and, where appropriate,
measures are also given in standard cups and spoons. Follow one set, but not a mixture,
because they are not interchangeable.

Printed and bound in Singapore

© Anness Publishing Limited 1997
Updated © 1999
3 5 7 9 10 8 6 4 2

Contents

$\mathscr{I}$NTRODUCTION

No other herb so vividly evokes a Mediterranean summer's day as basil, with its intense aroma and fresh, sweet taste. It speaks of sunshine and shimmering heat, of long, lazy lunches and ripe tomatoes bursting with flavour. The best-known variety is sweet basil, which has bright shiny green leaves and small white flowers; but there are almost sixty other varieties, each with its own distinctive flavour. Only the leaves are used for cooking; the stalks and flowers have almost no gastronomic value. It is only worth using fresh basil in cooking; dried basil is a poor substitute. Fortunately it is now possible to buy fresh basil from food stores all through the year.

Basil is one of the world's oldest herbs, native to Iran, India and South-East Asia, but now grown and enjoyed all over the world. From earliest times, it has been highly prized for both its culinary and medicinal qualities; the Romans regarded it as the king of herbs, naming it *basilicus* (the Latin form of the Greek word for king). From the Far East to the United States and Europe, basil has been incorporated into folklore.

"Holy" basil is the Hindu sacred herb, which is grown around temples and under altars as protection. This idea soon spread to Europe, where bunches of

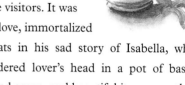

basil were hung in doorways to keep out evil spirits and other unwelcome visitors. It was also a symbol of love, immortalized by the poet Keats in his sad story of Isabella, who buried her murdered lover's head in a pot of basil, "whence thick, and green, and beautiful it grew, so that it smelt more balmy than its peers of Basil-tufts in Florence".

Above all, basil excels as a culinary herb. It is used extensively in Mediterranean and South-East Asian cooking, where several different varieties are often used in a single dish. It forms the basis of one of Italy's most famous exports, the wonderfully fragrant Genoese pesto sauce, and its French cousin, pistou. It has a special affinity with tomatoes; one of the best and simplest dishes in the world must be flavourful red tomatoes sliced and served with a drizzle of olive oil and a sprinkling of vibrant green basil leaves. It complements and enhances almost all salads and vegetables, and gives a special lift to mushrooms, eggs, poultry and delicate fish. Thanks to its sweet fragrance, basil can even be used in desserts; try adding a little to honey ice cream or a fruit-flavoured syrup for a wonderful, unexpected taste sensation.

Kate Whiteman

Types of Basil

Sweet Basil (*ocimum basilicum*)
Probably the finest and best-known of all the basils, sweet basil has an intense flavour and is perfect for use in classic Italian and Mediterranean cooking.

Lemon Basil (*ocimum basilicum var. citriodorum*)
This compact plant has a very distinctive, fragrant lemon flavour. It is delicious used raw in salad dressings or made into a refreshing tea, and is a classic ingredient in Indonesian cooking. Use it to add a citrus tang to fish or poultry.

Cinnamon Basil
The large, shiny leaves of this variety really do taste of cinnamon. The plant originally came from Mexico and is excellent with any type of spicy food.

Dark Opal Basil
The rather romantic name aptly describes the purplish-green colour of the leaves, which have a slightly gingery flavour and are robust enough to be used in sauces and stews. Don't try making pesto with dark opal basil, or you will end up with an unattractive brownish mixture.

Green Ruffles Basil
A beautiful plant, whose attractive leaves make it ideal for garnishes, as well as for salads and pasta dishes. It also comes in a bronze variety, "Purple Ruffles", which has a mild aniseed flavour.

Thai Basil (Anise Basil)
As its name suggests, this good-looking plant with dark serrated leaves tastes strongly of aniseed. It is used extensively in Thai dishes and is also good for flavouring salads and dressings. Unlike most basils, the flowers have the same flavour as the leaves, so they can be used as beautiful garnishes. This basil marries especially well with fish and seafood.

Purple Basil
This is a common variety of basil with the same rich, peppery flavour. It adds a dramatic flourish when added to green salad or tomato salad.

Neapolitana Basil
An Italian variety, with a powerful flavour, which is ideal to use for making pesto.

Dark opal basil

Green ruffles basil

Neapolitana basil

Lemon basil

Thai basil

Sweet basil

Cinnamon basil

Purple basil

$\mathcal{B}$ASIC $\mathcal{T}$ECHNIQUES

—— PREPARING BASIL ——

TEARING BASIL

Basil is best torn rather than chopped, since chopping tends to bruise the leaves and spoil the flavour. Tear the leaves into small pieces just before adding them to salads or dressings.

BASIL CHIFFONADE

Basil leaves can be shredded into fine ribbons to make an attractive garnish for salads or soups. Stack up four or five large leaves and roll them up tightly. Using a very sharp knife, shred the basil finely.

PURÉEING BASIL

To purée basil in a blender or food processor, or in a mortar, add a little liquid, such as oil, vinegar or water. Puréed basil can be spooned into ice cube trays and frozen for use in soups, stews and sauces.

PESTO

Pesto will keep in the fridge for several months, but it is also possible to freeze it. To do this, make the pesto in the usual way in a food processor or blender, but do not add the cheese. Freeze the pesto in small containers. Before use, thaw the pesto completely, then beat in Parmesan cheese just before serving.

—— BUYING, STORING AND GROWING BASIL ——

Nowadays, thanks to modern transport, it is possible to buy fresh basil all year round, either ready-cut in packets or growing in pots. Cut basil should be stored at 10°C, so keep it in a larder or other cool place; it will go black if you refrigerate it. Properly stored, cut basil will keep for two or three days. To keep it for longer, pack the leaves tightly into a jar and cover with olive oil. The leaves will soften, but can be used for any cooked dishes, and the oil makes the most delicious vinaigrette.

Don't freeze basil leaves; they turn brown and lose most of their flavour. If you must freeze it, make a purée and put it into ice cube trays. Once frozen, you can keep the cubes in freezer bags. Turn a summer glut into pesto, pistou, basil butter or basil oil. They will keep for several weeks.

In its native countries, basil is a perennial herb, but in more temperate climates, it becomes an annual. It is difficult to grow basil outdoors in colder countries, because it needs humidity and warmth, but it is easy to propagate on a sunny windowsill in your kitchen, which is convenient for cooking. To grow from seed, start it off under glass so that it has plenty of light and warmth. In cold weather, keep it away from the window. Water from the base, and with luck you will soon have an abundance of fresh basil to spice up your cooking.

BASIL OIL
Use sweet basil for this delicious oil.

You can enjoy the flavour of basil all year round by making basil-flavoured oil, which will add a special something to dressings and sauces. In a blender, combine 25g/1oz basil leaves, 150ml/¼ pint/⅔ cup extra virgin olive oil and salt and pepper to taste, and process for a couple of minutes. Pour into an airtight jar and keep in a cool place.

Makes about 150ml/¼ pint/⅔ cup

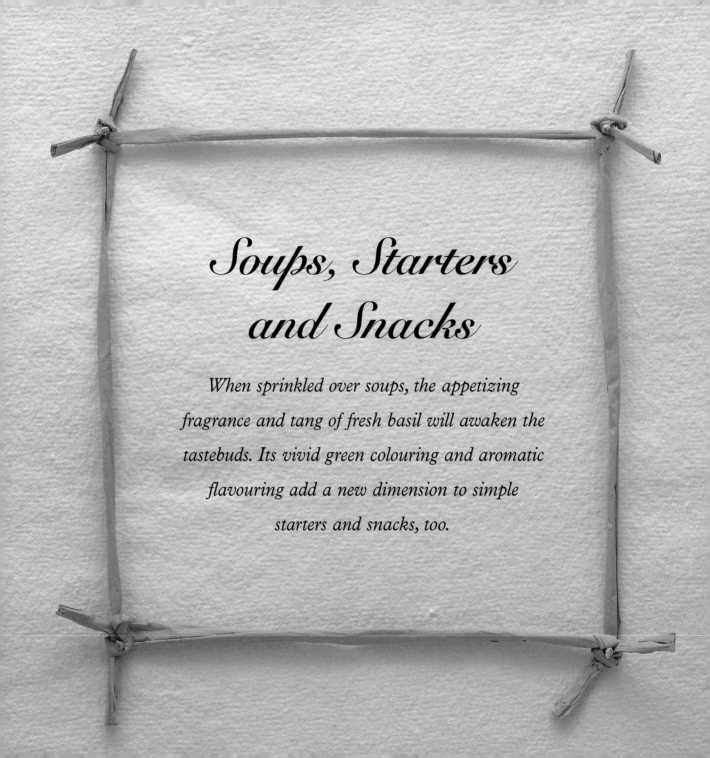

Soups, Starters and Snacks

When sprinkled over soups, the appetizing fragrance and tang of fresh basil will awaken the tastebuds. Its vivid green colouring and aromatic flavouring add a new dimension to simple starters and snacks, too.

TOMATO AND BASIL SOUP

The warm spicy flavour of basil complements tomatoes perfectly in this delicious soup.

Serves 4

30ml/2 tbsp olive oil

1 onion, chopped

2.5ml/½ tsp caster sugar

1 carrot, finely chopped

1 potato, finely chopped

1 garlic clove, crushed

675g/1½lb ripe tomatoes,
    roughly chopped

5ml/1 tsp tomato purée

1 bay leaf

1 thyme sprig

1 oregano sprig

4 basil leaves, roughly torn

300ml/½ pint/1¼ cups light chicken
    or vegetable stock

salt and ground black pepper

2–3 sun-dried tomatoes in oil and
    30ml/2 tbsp shredded fresh basil,
    to garnish

Heat the oil in a pan, add the onion and sprinkle with the sugar. Cook gently for 5 minutes, then add the carrot and potato. Cover and cook over a low heat for 10 minutes, without allowing the vegetables to brown.

Stir in the garlic, tomatoes, tomato purée, herbs and stock, with salt and pepper to taste. Cover and cook gently for 25–30 minutes, until the vegetables are tender.

Remove the pan from the heat and press the soup through a sieve, placed over a clean pan, to extract all the skins and pips. Taste and adjust the seasoning. Reheat the soup gently, then ladle into four warmed soup bowls. Finely chop the sun-dried tomatoes and mix with a little oil from the jar. Add a spoonful to each serving, then scatter the shredded basil over the top.

VEGETABLE SOUP WITH PISTOU

One of France's best-known specialities, Vegetable Soup with Pistou owes its flavour to Provençal produce and homemade basil pesto.

Serves 4–6

1 courgette, diced
1 small potato, diced
1 shallot, chopped
1 carrot, diced
225g/8oz can chopped tomatoes
1.2 litres/2 pints/5 cups
*   vegetable stock*
50g/2oz French beans, cut into
*   1cm/½in lengths*
50g/2oz/½ cup frozen petits pois
50g/2oz/½ cup small pasta shapes
60–90ml/4–6 tbsp homemade or
*   bought pesto*
15ml/1 tbsp sun-dried tomato paste
salt and ground black pepper
freshly grated Parmesan cheese,
*   to serve*

Place the courgette, potato, shallot, carrot and tomatoes in a large saucepan. Add the vegetable stock and season with salt and pepper. Bring to the boil, then lower the heat, cover and simmer for 20 minutes.

Add the French beans, petits pois and pasta. Cook for 10 minutes more, until the pasta is tender. Adjust the seasoning.

Ladle the soup into warmed individual bowls. Mix together the pesto and sun-dried tomato paste, and stir a spoonful into each serving. Serve with grated Parmesan cheese to sprinkle into each bowl.

MELON AND BASIL SOUP

In this chilled soup, vivid green basil provides a pleasing contrast to the pale shade of the melon.

Serves 4–6

2 charentais melons or cantaloupes
75g/3oz/⅓ cup caster sugar
finely grated rind and juice of 1 lime
45ml/3 tbsp shredded fresh basil
fresh basil leaves, to garnish

COOK'S TIP
Add the syrup in two stages, as the amount of sugar needed will depend on the sweetness of the melons.

Cut the melons in half, scrape out the seeds and throw them away. Using a melon baller, scoop out 20–24 balls and set aside for the garnish. Scoop out the remaining flesh into a blender or food processor.

Place the caster sugar and lime rind in a small saucepan, then pour in 175ml/6fl oz/¾ cup water and place the pan over a low heat. Stir until the sugar has dissolved, then bring to the boil. Lower the heat and simmer for 2–3 minutes. Cool slightly, then pour half the mixture into the blender or food processor with the melon flesh. Blend until smooth, adding the remaining syrup and lime juice to taste.

Pour the mixture into a serving bowl, stir in the shredded basil and chill. Serve garnished with basil leaves and the reserved melon balls.

TOMATO, BASIL AND BREAD SALAD

Basil adds delicious flavour to this traditional peasant dish from Tuscany. It was originally created to use up bread that was several days old.

Serves 4

400g/14oz/3½ cups stale white or
*   brown bread or rolls*
4 large tomatoes
1 large onion, or 6 spring onions
handful of basil leaves, to serve

For the dressing

60ml/4 tbsp extra virgin olive oil
30ml/2 tbsp white wine vinegar
salt and ground black pepper

Cut the bread or rolls into thick slices. Place in a shallow bowl, and soak with cold water. Leave for at least 30 minutes.

Cut the tomatoes into chunks. Place in a serving bowl. Finely slice the onion or spring onions, and add to the tomatoes. Squeeze the water out of the bread and add the bread to the onions and tomatoes.

Make a dressing with the oil and vinegar. Season with salt and black pepper. Pour it over the salad and mix well. Allow to stand in a cool place for at least 2 hours then serve, sprinkled with basil leaves.

SMOKED SALMON PANCAKES WITH BASIL PESTO

Mini pesto-flavoured pancakes are topped with crème fraîche, smoked salmon and fresh basil to create this delicious bite-size starter.

Makes 12–16

120ml/4fl oz/½ cup milk
125g/4oz/1 cup self-raising flour
1 egg
30ml/2 tbsp homemade or
  bought pesto
vegetable oil, for frying
200ml/7fl oz/scant 1 cup
  crème fraîche
75g/3oz smoked salmon
15g/½oz/1 tbsp pine nuts, toasted
12–16 fresh basil sprigs, to garnish

Pour half of the milk into a mixing bowl. Add the flour, egg and pesto. Mix to a smooth batter, then add the rest of the milk and stir until it is evenly blended.

Heat the vegetable oil in a large frying pan. Spoon the pancake mixture into the heated oil in small heaps. Allow about 30 seconds for the pancakes to rise, then turn and cook briefly on the other side. Continue cooking the pancakes in batches until all the batter is used up.

Arrange the pancakes on a serving plate and top each one with a spoonful of crème fraîche. Cut the salmon into 1cm/½in strips and place on top of each pancake. Add a scattering of pine nuts and garnish each pancake with a fresh basil sprig.

COOK'S TIP
The pancakes are ready for turning when tiny bubbles appear on the surface.

FRIED CLAMS WITH BASIL AND CHILLIES

This delectable combination of clams, basil and chillies comes from Thailand, where it can often be found on the menu at seaside restaurants.

Serves 4

1kg/2¼lb fresh clams
30ml/2 tbsp vegetable oil
4 garlic cloves, finely chopped
15ml/1 tbsp grated fresh root ginger
4 shallots, finely chopped
30ml/2 tbsp yellow bean sauce
6 red chillies, seeded and chopped
15ml/1 tbsp fish sauce
pinch of granulated sugar
1 handful of basil leaves, plus extra
*   to garnish*

COOK'S TIP
Fresh clams are usually
available all year round, but
you may need to order them

from the fishmonger.

Wash and scrub the clams. Heat the oil in a wok or large frying pan. Add the garlic and ginger and fry for 30 seconds, then add the shallots and fry for 1–2 minutes more.

Add the clams. Using a fish slice or spatula, turn them a few times to coat with the oil. Stir in the yellow bean sauce and half the red chillies.

Continue to cook, stirring often, for 5–7 minutes, or until all the clams open. You may need to add a splash of water. Adjust the seasoning with fish sauce and a little sugar.

Finally, add the basil and transfer to individual warmed bowls or a platter. Garnish with the remaining red chillies and basil leaves.

MOZZARELLA, TOMATO AND BASIL SALAD

This salad is considered patriotic in Italy, as its prime ingredients match the national flag: red, green and white. Choose tomatoes similar in size to the mozzarella cheese.

Serves 4

4 large tomatoes
400g/14oz/2 cups mozzarella cheese
8–10 fresh basil leaves
60ml/4 tbsp extra virgin olive oil
salt and ground black pepper

COOK'S TIP
In Italy the most sought-after mozzarella is made from the milk of water buffalo. It is found mainly in the south and in Campania, and, like tomatoes, has a real affinity for the flavour of basil.

Slice the tomatoes and mozzarella into neat thick rounds. Arrange in overlapping slices on a serving dish, tucking the basil leaves between the slices or scattering them over the top.

Drizzle the salad with olive oil and sprinkle with a little salt. Serve with the black pepper passed round separately.

PRAWN "POPCORN" WITH BASIL MAYONNAISE

One of the most compelling reasons for visiting Louisiana is to taste the wonderful Cajun cooking. This dish of spiced prawns and basil mayonnaise comes from there and it is truly irresistible.

Serves 8

900g/2lb raw prawns, peeled
*   and deveined*
2 eggs, beaten
250ml/8fl oz/1 cup dry white wine
50g/2oz/½ cup fine cornmeal
50g/2oz/½ cup plain flour
15ml/1 tbsp finely snipped
*   fresh chives*
1 garlic clove, crushed
2.5ml/½ tsp fresh thyme leaves
1.5ml/¼ tsp salt
1.5ml/¼ tsp cayenne pepper
1.5ml/¼ tsp ground black pepper
oil, for deep-frying

For the mayonnaise

1 egg yolk
10ml/2 tsp Dijon mustard
15ml/1 tbsp white wine vinegar
250ml/8fl oz/1 cup olive oil
25g/1oz/½ cup fresh basil leaves,
*   finely shredded*
salt and ground black pepper

Rinse the prawns in a sieve under cold running water. Drain well and set aside in a cool place. Mix the eggs and wine in a small bowl.

In a mixing bowl, combine the cornmeal and flour, chives, garlic, thyme, salt, cayenne and pepper. Gradually whisk in the egg mixture to make a smooth batter. Cover and leave to stand for 1 hour at room temperature.

Make the mayonnaise. Combine the egg yolk, mustard and vinegar in a mixing bowl. Add salt and pepper to taste. Add the oil in a thin stream, beating vigorously with a wire whisk. When the mixture is thick and smooth, stir in the basil. Cover and chill until ready to serve.

Heat oil to a depth of 5–7.5cm/2–3in in a large frying pan or deep-fryer to about 185°C/360°F, or until a small piece of dry bread sizzles as soon as it is added to the pan. Dip the prawns into the batter and fry in small batches for 2–3 minutes, or until golden brown. Turn as necessary for even colouring. Remove with a slotted spoon and drain on kitchen paper. Serve hot, with the basil mayonnaise.

TOMATO AND BASIL TARTS

These crisp little tartlets are easy to make and, as ever, basil and tomato make a winning combination.

Serves 4

2 sheets of filo pastry

1 egg white

75g/3oz/scant ½ cup cream cheese

1 handful of fresh basil leaves

3 small tomatoes, sliced

salt and ground black pepper

Preheat the oven to 200°C/400°F/Gas 6. Brush the sheets of filo pastry lightly with egg white and cut into sixteen 10cm/4in squares.

Place the squares in eight muffin tins, using a double layer each time. Beat the cheese until it is creamy, then divide it among the filo cases. Season with black pepper and top with basil leaves.

Arrange the tomato slices on the tarts, add salt and pepper to taste, and bake for 10–12 minutes, until golden. Serve warm, fresh from the oven.

COOK'S TIP

Egg white has been used for the filo pastry in order to cut down on the amount of fat in the tarts. Use melted butter or oil, if you prefer.

GNOCCHI WITH BASIL BUTTER SAUCE

Italian spinach and cheese dumplings make a treat when served with a buttery lemon and basil sauce.

Serves 4

175g/6oz/1¼ cups cold
   mashed potato
75g/3oz/½ cup semolina
115g/4oz/1 cup frozen leaf spinach,
   thawed, squeezed dry and chopped
115g/4oz/½ cup ricotta cheese
25g/1oz/⅓ cup grated Parmesan
   cheese, plus extra for sprinkling
30ml/2 tbsp beaten egg
2.5ml/½ tsp salt
generous pinch of grated nutmeg
ground black pepper
fresh basil sprigs, to garnish

For the butter

75g/3oz/6 tbsp butter
5ml/1 tsp grated lemon rind
15ml/1 tbsp lemon juice
15ml/1 tbsp finely shredded
   fresh basil

Preheat the oven to 140°C/275°F/Gas 1. Grease a dish and place in the oven. Mix all the gnocchi ingredients except the basil. Roll a piece of the mixture along the prongs of a fork until ridged. Repeat with the remaining mixture to make 28 gnocchi. Place on a baking sheet lined with clear film.

Bring a large pan of water to the boil, reduce the heat slightly, and drop the gnocchi into the simmering water. They will sink to the bottom at first, but after about 2 minutes they will rise to the surface. Simmer for 1 minute more, then remove with a slotted spoon and transfer to the warmed dish. Keep hot in the oven while cooking successive batches. Preheat the grill.

When all the gnocchi are cooked, sprinkle with Parmesan. Grill under a high heat for 2 minutes, or until lightly browned. Meanwhile, melt the butter and stir in the lemon rind and juice with the basil and seasoning. Serve the gnocchi with the hot butter poured on top and garnished with basil.

GUACAMOLE, BASIL AND TOMATO PITTA POCKETS

This is a favourite family recipe – the fresh basil and tomato are perfect with the spicy guacamole.

Serves 6

6 large pitta breads

2 beefsteak tomatoes, sliced

12 fresh basil leaves

2 large ripe avocados

1 tomato

½ red onion

1 garlic clove, crushed

15ml/1 tbsp fresh lime juice

1.5ml/¼ tsp chilli powder

30ml/2 tbsp chopped fresh dill

Slice open the ends of the pitta breads to make pockets. Place 1–2 slices of tomato and 2 basil leaves in each one.

Cut the avocados in half, remove the stones and peel, then chop the flesh roughly. Chop the remaining tomato and the red onion. Mix the garlic, lime juice, chilli powder and dill in a salad bowl, add the chopped avocado, tomato and onion and stir gently.

Fill the pitta pockets with the avocado mixture and serve immediately.

COOK'S TIP

Warm the pitta breads before filling them, if you like. Place the six breads between sheets of kitchen paper and heat them in the microwave on High for 2–2½ minutes.

SAFFRON AND BASIL BREADSTICKS

Serve these basil-flavoured snacks solo, or with a dipping sauce such as taramasalata or tzatziki.

Makes 32

generous pinch of saffron strands
450g/1lb/4 cups strong white flour
5ml/1 tsp salt
10ml/2 tsp easy-blend dried yeast
45ml/3 tbsp olive oil
45ml/3 tbsp finely shredded
*   fresh basil*

VARIATION
For sesame sticks, omit the saffron. Brush the risen breadsticks lightly with beaten egg and roll in sesame seeds before baking.

Put the saffron strands in a small bowl. Pour in 30ml/2 tbsp hot water and leave to infuse for 10 minutes.

Sift the flour and salt into a large bowl. Stir in the yeast, then make a well in the centre of the dry ingredients. Pour in 300ml/½ pint/1¼ cups lukewarm water and the strained saffron liquid and mix in a little of the flour. Add the oil and basil and continue to mix to a soft dough.

Turn out the dough and knead it on a lightly floured surface for about 10 minutes until smooth and elastic. Place in a greased bowl, cover with clear film and leave for about 1 hour until it has doubled in bulk.

Preheat the oven to 220°C/425°F/Gas 7 and grease 2–3 baking sheets. Knead the dough for 2–3 minutes and shape into 32 long sticks. Place well apart on the baking sheets, then leave for 15–30 minutes, or until they become puffy. Bake for 15 minutes until crisp and golden. Serve warm.

27

Seafood, Poultry and Meat Dishes

Sweet basil comes into its own when used as part of a marinade or sauce – it perfectly complements all sorts of seafood, poultry and meat – or try Thai basil for an authentic taste of South-East Asia.

PRAWN CURRY WITH BASIL

This is a fragrant and creamy green curry where basil contributes greatly to the colour and flavour.

Serves 4–6

30ml/2 tbsp vegetable oil

30ml/2 tbsp green curry paste

450g/1lb raw king prawns, peeled
   and deveined

4 kaffir lime leaves, torn

1 lemon grass stalk, bruised
   and chopped

250ml/8fl oz/1 cup coconut milk

30ml/2 tbsp fish sauce

½ cucumber, seeded and cut into
   thin batons

10–15 fresh basil leaves

4 green chillies, seeded and sliced,
   to garnish

VARIATION
Thin strips of boneless, skinless chicken breasts can be used instead of prawns, if liked.

Heat the oil in a frying pan. Add the green curry paste and fry until bubbling and fragrant. Add the prawns, kaffir lime leaves and lemon grass. Fry for 1–2 minutes, until the prawns are pink.

Stir in the coconut milk and bring to a gentle boil. Lower the heat slightly and simmer, stirring occasionally, for about 5 minutes, or until the prawns are tender.

Stir in the fish sauce, cucumber and basil leaves, sprinkle with the green chillies and serve.

PLAICE AND PESTO PARCELS

Opening these parcels is pure pleasure as a heavenly aroma of basil and lemon escapes.

Serves 4

75g/3oz/6 tbsp butter

20ml/4 tsp homemade or
   bought pesto

8 small plaice fillets, skinned

1 small fennel bulb, cut
   into matchsticks

2 small carrots, cut into matchsticks

2 courgettes, cut into matchsticks

10ml/2 tsp finely grated lemon rind

vegetable oil, for brushing

salt and ground black pepper

fresh basil leaves, to garnish

COOK'S TIP

Take the parcels hot from the oven to the table – the greaseproof paper becomes translucent when baked and looks very attractive.

Preheat the oven to 190°C/375°F/Gas 5. Beat three-quarters of the butter with the pesto and season to taste. Spread the pesto butter over the skinned side of each plaice fillet and roll up from the thick end.

Melt the remaining butter in a small saucepan, add the fennel and carrots and sauté for 3 minutes. Add the courgettes and cook for 2 minutes. Remove from the heat and add the lemon rind, with salt and pepper to taste.

Cut four squares of greaseproof paper, each large enough to enclose two plaice rolls. Brush with oil. Spoon a quarter of the vegetables into the centre of each, then arrange two plaice rolls on top. Seal the parcels tightly and place in a roasting tin. Bake for 15–20 minutes, until the fish is just tender.

To serve, open the parcels, sprinkle with the basil leaves and grind over a little black pepper.

HALIBUT WITH BASIL SALSA

Freshly grilled halibut fillets served with a tangy tomato and basil salsa make a perfect summertime dinner. Just sit back and let your tastebuds enjoy the treat.

Serves 4

*4 halibut fillets, about 175g/6oz
    each, skinned*

45ml/3 tbsp olive oil

salt and ground black pepper

For the salsa

1 tomato, roughly chopped

¼ red onion, finely chopped

*1 small drained canned
    jalapeño chilli*

30ml/2 tbsp balsamic vinegar

10 large fresh basil leaves

15ml/1 tbsp olive oil

COOK'S TIP

*This is delicious barbecued.
Cook it in a hinged grill and
take care when basting as olive
oil dripped on to the coals will
cause flare-ups.*

Make the salsa. Mix the tomato, red onion, jalapeño chilli and balsamic vinegar in a bowl.

Shred the basil leaves finely, and stir them into the tomato salsa, with the olive oil. Add salt and pepper to taste. Cover and leave to marinate for at least 3 hours.

Rub the halibut fillets with olive oil, salt and pepper. Preheat the grill. Cook the halibut for about 4 minutes on each side, depending on the thickness. Baste with olive oil as necessary. Serve with the salsa.

PAN-FRIED RED MULLET WITH BASIL AND CITRUS FRUITS

Red mullet is popular throughout the Mediterranean and this Italian recipe combines it with anchovies, oranges, lemons and basil for an unusual taste sensation.

Serves 4

4 red mullet, about 225g/8oz
*   each, filleted*
90ml/6 tbsp olive oil
10 peppercorns, crushed
2 oranges, 1 peeled and sliced and
*   1 squeezed*
1 lemon
15g/¹/₂oz/2 tbsp plain flour
15g/¹/₂oz/1 tbsp butter
2 drained canned anchovies, chopped
60ml/4 tbsp shredded fresh basil
salt and ground black pepper

Place the fish fillets in a single layer in a shallow dish. Pour over the olive oil and sprinkle with the crushed peppercorns. Lay the orange slices on top of the fish. Cover the dish, and leave it to marinate in the fridge for at least 4 hours.

Cut the lemon in half. Remove the skin and pith from one half using a small sharp knife, and slice thinly. Squeeze the juice from the other half.

Lift the fish out of the marinade, and pat dry on kitchen paper. Reserve the marinade and orange slices. Season the fish with salt and pepper and dust lightly with flour.

Heat 45ml/3 tbsp of the reserved marinade in a large frying pan. Add the fish and fry for 2 minutes on each side. Remove from the pan and keep hot. Discard the marinade that is left in the pan.

Melt the butter in the pan with the remaining original marinade. Add the anchovies and cook until they begin to disintegrate. Stir in the orange and lemon juice, then check the seasoning and simmer until slightly reduced. Stir in the basil. Pour the sauce over the fish and garnish with the reserved orange and lemon slices.

COOK'S TIP

If you prefer, use other fish fillets for this dish, such as lemon sole, haddock or hake.

CHICKEN WITH RED PESTO

Rich, robust flavours and strong colours topped with a basil garnish make this a memorable dish.

Serves 4

15g/½oz/2 tbsp plain flour

4 chicken legs, breasts or quarters

30ml/2 tbsp olive oil

1 onion, chopped

2 garlic cloves, chopped

1 red pepper, seeded and chopped

400g/14oz can chopped tomatoes

30ml/2 tbsp red pesto

4 sun-dried tomatoes in oil, chopped

150ml/¼ pint/⅔ cup chicken stock

5ml/1 tsp dried oregano

8 black olives, stoned

salt and ground black pepper

chopped fresh basil and basil leaves,
   to garnish

tagliatelle, to serve

Mix the flour with salt and pepper in a plastic bag. Add the chicken, close the bag tightly and shake until coated. Heat the oil in a flameproof casserole, add the chicken and brown quickly. Remove and set aside.

Lower the heat slightly and add the onion, garlic and red pepper. Cook for 5 minutes, then stir in the tomatoes, pesto, sun-dried tomatoes, stock and oregano. Bring to the boil.

Return the chicken to the casserole, season lightly, cover and simmer for 30–35 minutes, or until the chicken is cooked.

Add the olives and simmer for 5 minutes more. Transfer to a warmed serving dish, sprinkle with the chopped basil and garnish with basil leaves. Serve with hot tagliatelle.

STIR-FRIED CHICKEN WITH BASIL

The spicy, sharp flavour of Thai basil is the secret ingredient in this wonderful dish.

Serves 4–6

45ml/3 tbsp vegetable oil

4 garlic cloves, sliced

2–4 red chillies, seeded and chopped

450g/1lb chicken, cut into
* bite-size pieces*

30–45ml/2–3 tbsp fish sauce

10ml/2 tsp dark soy sauce

5ml/1 tsp sugar

10–12 fresh Thai basil leaves

To garnish

2 red chillies, finely sliced

20 deep fried Thai basil leaves
* (see Cook's Tip)*

COOK'S TIP

To deep fry Thai basil leaves,
make sure they are completely
dry. Deep fry in hot oil for
about 30–40 seconds, lift out
and drain on kitchen paper.

Heat the oil in a wok or large frying pan, swirling it around carefully to coat the entire cooking surface. Add the garlic and red chillies and stir-fry until golden.

Add the chicken to the wok or pan; stir-fry until it changes colour.

Season with fish sauce, soy sauce and sugar. Continue to stir-fry for about 3–4 minutes, or until the chicken is cooked. Stir in the fresh Thai basil leaves. Garnish with sliced chillies and deep fried basil.

ROAST LEG OF LAMB WITH BASIL PESTO

For this American speciality, lamb is marinated and baked under a fragrant basil blanket.

Serves 6

115g/4oz/2 cups fresh basil leaves
4 garlic cloves, roughly chopped
45ml/3 tbsp pine nuts
150ml/¼ pint/⅔ cup olive oil
50g/2oz/⅔ cup freshly grated
   Parmesan cheese
5ml/1 tsp salt, or to taste
1 leg of lamb, about 2.5kg/5½lb
cooked vegetables, to serve

Start by making the pesto. Combine the basil, garlic and pine nuts in a food processor or blender and process until finely chopped. With the motor running, slowly add the oil in a steady stream through the feeder tube. Scrape the mixture into a bowl. Stir in the Parmesan and salt.

Place the lamb in a roasting tin. Make several slits in the meat with a sharp knife and spoon some pesto into each slit. Rub more pesto over the surface of the lamb. Continue patting on the pesto in a thick, even layer. Cover and allow to stand for 2 hours at room temperature, or overnight in the fridge.

Preheat the oven to 180°C/350°F/Gas 4. Transfer the roasting tin to the oven and roast the lamb, allowing about 20 minutes per 450g/1lb for rare meat and 25 minutes per 450g/1lb for medium-rare. Turn the lamb occasionally during roasting.

Remove the lamb from the oven, cover it loosely with tented foil, and allow to rest for about 15 minutes before carving and serving with a selection of vegetables.

COOK'S TIP
Buy Parmesan in the piece
and grate it yourself. The
flavour will be superior to the
pre-grated packed product.

TURKEY WITH BASIL AND PEPPER SAUCE

Turkey rolled up with a garlic and basil cream and served with a pepper sauce is a popular supper treat.

Serves 4

4 turkey escalopes

*75g/3oz Boursin or garlic-flavoured
cream cheese*

12 fresh basil leaves

25g/1oz/2 tbsp butter

15ml/1 tbsp olive oil

salt and ground black pepper

For the yellow pepper sauce

15ml/1 tbsp olive oil

*2 large yellow peppers, seeded
and chopped*

1 small onion, chopped

15ml/1 tbsp fresh orange juice

300ml/½ pint/1¼ cups chicken stock

COOK'S TIP

*Skinless, boneless chicken
breasts or veal escalopes could
be used instead of the turkey.*

Make the yellow pepper sauce. Heat the oil in a saucepan and gently fry the peppers and onion until beginning to soften. Add the orange juice and stock and cook until the vegetables are very soft.

Meanwhile, lay the turkey escalopes on a board and beat them out lightly. Spread the escalopes with the cream cheese. Shred half the basil leaves and sprinkle on top, then roll up each escalope, tucking in the ends like an envelope, and secure neatly with half a cocktail stick.

Melt the butter with the oil in a frying pan. Fry the turkey rolls for about 7–8 minutes, turning them frequently, until golden and cooked.

Meanwhile, press the pepper mixture through a sieve until smooth, then return to a clean pan. Season the sauce to taste and warm through, or serve cold, with the escalopes, garnished with the remaining basil leaves.

BEEF, AUBERGINE AND BASIL CURRY

Tender strips of beef are prepared in a green curry sauce with fresh basil in this exquisite Thai curry.

Serves 4–6

15ml/1 tbsp vegetable oil

600ml/1 pint/2½ cups coconut milk

450g/1lb sirloin of beef

150g/5oz small Thai aubergines

4 kaffir lime leaves, torn

15–30ml/1–2 tbsp fish sauce

5ml/1 tsp palm sugar

small handful of Thai basil leaves

green chillies, to garnish (optional)

For the green curry paste

15 hot green chillies

2 lemon grass stalks, chopped

3 shallots, sliced

2 garlic cloves

15ml/1 tbsp chopped galangal

4 kaffir lime leaves, chopped

5ml/1 tsp chopped coriander root

6 black peppercorns

5ml/1 tsp coriander seeds, roasted

5ml/1 tsp cumin seeds, roasted

15ml/1 tbsp sugar

5ml/1 tsp salt

30ml/2 tbsp vegetable oil

Combine all the curry paste ingredients, except the oil, in a mortar, food processor or blender. Blend to a paste, then add the oil, a little at a time. Scrape the paste into a glass jar and store in the fridge until required.

Heat the oil in a wok. Add 45ml/3 tbsp of the green curry paste and fry until fragrant, then stir in half the coconut milk, a little at a time. Cook for about 5–6 minutes, until an oily sheen appears on the surface of the mixture.

Meanwhile, cut the beef into long thin slices and the aubergines in half lengthways. Add the beef to the saucepan with the kaffir lime leaves, fish sauce, sugar and aubergines. Cook for 2–3 minutes, then stir in the remaining coconut milk. Bring back to a simmer and cook until the meat and aubergines are tender. Stir in the Thai basil leaves just before serving. Garnish the curry with slices of green chillies, if liked.

Pastries, Pizzas, Pasta and Rice

Fragrant basil leaves add the true taste of Italy to any pizza or pasta dish, and transform the simplest rice dish into something special. Sweet basil is perfect in risotto, while purple basil and Thai rice offer an exotic combination.

COURGETTE AND BASIL QUICHE

If possible, use a hard goat's cheese for this flan as its flavour complements the courgettes and basil.

Serves 6

115g/4oz/scant 1 cup wholemeal flour

115g/4oz/1 cup plain flour

115g/4oz/½ cup butter or margarine

For the filling

30ml/2 tbsp olive oil

1 red onion, thinly sliced

2 large courgettes, sliced

175g/6oz/1½ cups grated cheese

30ml/2 tbsp shredded fresh basil

3 eggs, beaten

300ml/½ pint/1¼ cups milk

salt and ground black pepper

COOK'S TIP

To bake blind, line the pastry case with greaseproof paper and fill it with baking beans. Bake for the time specified, removing paper and beans for the final 5 minutes to crisp the base.

Preheat the oven to 200°C/400°F/Gas 6. Mix the flours together in a large bowl. Rub in the butter or margarine until the mixture resembles breadcrumbs, then mix to a firm dough with cold water. Roll out the pastry and use it to line a 23–25cm/9–10in flan tin. Prick the base, chill for 30 minutes, then bake blind for 20 minutes. Remove the flan case from the oven. Turn the heat down to 180°C/350°F/Gas 4.

Heat the oil in a frying pan and sweat the onion for 5 minutes until soft. Add the courgettes and fry for 5 minutes. Spoon the onion and courgettes into the pastry case. Scatter over most of the cheese and all of the basil.

Beat the eggs and milk with salt and pepper to taste. Pour over the filling. Top with the remaining cheese. Bake the flan for about 40 minutes, or until risen and just firm to the touch in the centre. Cool slightly before serving.

RICOTTA AND BASIL TART

Rich and creamy, this basil-scented tart makes the perfect centrepiece for a summer buffet.

Serves 8–10
150g/5oz/1¼ cups plain flour
2.5ml/½ tsp salt
75g/3oz/6 tbsp butter
75g/3oz/6 tbsp margarine

For the filling
50g/2oz/2 cups basil leaves
25g/1oz/1 cup flat leaf parsley
120ml/4fl oz/½ cup extra virgin
   olive oil
2 eggs, beaten, plus 1 egg yolk
800g/1¾ lb/3½ cups ricotta cheese
50g/2oz/½ cup black olives, stoned
50g/2oz/½ cup grated
   Parmesan cheese
salt and ground black pepper

Combine the flour and salt in a bowl. Rub in the butter and margarine until the mixture resembles coarse breadcrumbs. Stir in just enough iced water to bind the dough. Gather into a ball, wrap and chill for at least 20 minutes.

Preheat the oven to 190°C/375°F/Gas 5. Roll out the dough thinly and line a 25cm/10in tart tin. Prick the base, then bake blind for 12 minutes. Remove the paper and weights and bake for about 3–5 minutes until golden. Turn the heat down to 180°C/350°F/Gas 4.

Mix the basil, parsley and olive oil in a food processor or blender. Season well with salt and pepper and process until finely chopped.

Whisk the eggs and yolk, gently fold in the ricotta, then fold in the basil mixture and olives. Stir in the Parmesan and adjust the seasoning. Pour the filling into the pastry case and bake for 30–35 minutes until set. Serve warm.

TOMATO AND BASIL QUICK PIZZA

This quick-and-easy pizza owes its popularity to the classic flavourful duo of tomatoes and basil.

Serves 6–8

*175g/6oz shortcrust pastry, thawed
 if frozen*
30ml/2 tbsp extra virgin olive oil
*175g/6oz/1 cup mozzarella cheese,
 thinly sliced*
12 fresh basil leaves
*4–5 tomatoes, cut into
 5mm/¼in slices*
60ml/4 tbsp grated Parmesan cheese
salt and ground black pepper

COOK'S TIP
*A scone crust makes a good
quick pizza base, too.*

Preheat the oven to 190°C/375°F/Gas 5. Roll out the pastry thinly and line a 28cm/11in pizza or pie tin, trimming the edges evenly. Chill for 20 minutes. Prick the base, then bake blind for 12 minutes. Remove the paper and weights and bake for 3–5 minutes more.

Remove the pastry case from the oven but leave the oven on. Brush the pastry with a little of the oil. Line with the mozzarella. Tear half of the basil leaves into pieces and sprinkle on top.

Arrange the tomato slices over the cheese. Dot with the remaining whole basil leaves. Sprinkle with salt and pepper and Parmesan and drizzle with the remaining oil. Bake for about 35 minutes. If the cheese exudes a lot of liquid during baking, tilt the pan and spoon it off to keep the pastry from becoming soggy. Serve hot or at room temperature.

VEGETABLE PIZZA WITH BASIL

Use any combination of colourful fresh vegetables on this scrumptious pizza. A sizzling golden mozzarella and basil topping ensures it's a big hit with the whole family.

Serves 4

400g/14oz can peeled plum
*   tomatoes, drained*
2 broccoli spears
225g/8oz fresh asparagus spears
2 small courgettes
75ml/5 tbsp olive oil
50g/2oz/½ cup frozen peas, thawed
4 spring onions, sliced
28cm/11in ready-to-bake pizza
*   base, homemade or bought*
75g/3oz/½ cup mozzarella cheese,
*   cut into small dice*
10 fresh basil leaves, torn in pieces
2 garlic cloves, finely chopped
salt and ground black pepper

Preheat the oven to 240°C/475°F/Gas 9 for at least 20 minutes before baking the pizza. Purée the tomatoes in a blender or food processor, or press them through a strainer into a bowl.

Peel the broccoli stems and asparagus. Bring a saucepan of water to the boil, add the broccoli, asparagus and courgettes and boil for 4–5 minutes. Drain and cut the vegetables into bite-size pieces.

Heat 30ml/2 tbsp of the olive oil in a small saucepan. Stir in the thawed peas and spring onions, and cook for 5–6 minutes, stirring frequently. Remove from the heat.

Spread the puréed tomatoes on the pizza dough, leaving the rim uncovered. Add the blanched and sautéed vegetables, arranging them neatly and evenly over the tomatoes.

Sprinkle with the mozzarella, basil, garlic, salt and pepper, and drizzle with the remaining olive oil. Bake for about 20 minutes, or until the crust is golden brown and the cheese has melted.

PASTA WITH VEGETABLES AND BASIL

This colourful sauce makes the most of new crops of fresh tender spring vegetables, scented with basil.

Serves 6

1–2 small young carrots

2 spring onions

1 courgette

2 tomatoes

75g/3oz/ ½ cup green beans

1 yellow pepper, seeded

75g/3oz/ ¾ cup frozen peas, thawed

60ml/4 tbsp olive oil

25g/1oz/2 tbsp butter

1 garlic clove, finely chopped

5–6 fresh basil leaves, torn into pieces

500g/1¼lb/5 cups dried pasta shapes

salt and ground black pepper

basil leaves, to garnish

grated Parmesan cheese, to serve

COOK'S TIP

Any pasta shapes can be used:
try fusilli, penne or farfalle.
Spinach or tomato coloured
pasta also looks very effective.

Cut all the vegetables except the peas into bite-size pieces. Heat the oil and butter in a large frying pan. Add the chopped vegetables and peas, and cook over a medium heat for 5–6 minutes, stirring occasionally. Add the garlic and the basil leaves and season with salt and pepper. Cover and cook for 5–8 minutes more, or until the vegetables are just tender.

Meanwhile, bring a large saucepan of lightly salted water to the boil. Add the pasta and cook for the time stated on the packet, until just tender. Before draining it, reserve a cupful of the pasta water.

Turn the drained pasta into the pan with the sauce, and mix well. If the sauce seems too dry, add a few spoonfuls of the reserved pasta water. Serve the Parmesan separately. Garnish the pasta with basil leaves.

SPAGHETTI WITH BACON AND BASIL SAUCE

The heat from the pasta releases the aromatic flavour of basil in this delicious dish.

Serves 4

*50g/2oz/2 cups finely shredded
    fresh basil*
2 garlic cloves, crushed
60ml/4 tbsp pine nuts, toasted
150ml/¼ pint/⅔ cup olive oil
350g/12oz dried spaghetti
*4 rindless smoked streaky bacon
    rashers, chopped*
1 onion, finely chopped
*60ml/4 tbsp freshly grated
    Parmesan cheese*
salt and ground black pepper
fresh basil leaves, to garnish

COOK'S TIP

*For extra flavour, drizzle a
dash of Worcestershire sauce
over the bacon mixture before
adding it to the pasta. It tastes
wonderful with the basil sauce.*

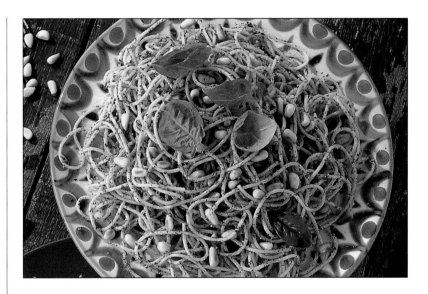

Put the basil, garlic and half the pine nuts into a food processor or blender. With the motor running slowly, gradually add the oil and process to a thick purée.

Bring a large saucepan of lightly salted water to the boil. Add the spaghetti and cook for the time stated on the packet, until just tender.

Meanwhile, heat the bacon in a frying pan until the fat runs, then add the onion and fry until the bacon is crisp and the onion tender.

Transfer the basil purée to a large warm bowl. Drain the spaghetti thoroughly and add it to the bowl with the bacon mixture and the Parmesan cheese. Toss well to coat. Sprinkle over the remaining pine nuts and the basil leaves and serve immediately.

PASTA AND PESTO

There is nothing more evocative of the warmth of Italy than a good homemade basil pesto. Serve generous spoonfuls of this one with your favourite pasta.

Serves 3–4

50g/2oz/2 cups basil leaves

2 garlic cloves, crushed

30ml/2 tbsp pine nuts

120ml/4fl oz/ ½ cup olive oil

40g/1½oz/ ½ cup finely grated
*   Parmesan cheese*

350g/12oz tagliatelle

salt and ground black pepper

basil sprigs, to garnish

Using a pestle and mortar, grind the basil, garlic and pine nuts to a fine paste. Transfer the mixture to a bowl and whisk in the oil, a little at a time. Add the cheese and mix well. Add salt and pepper to taste.

Alternatively, place the basil, garlic and pine nuts in a food processor or blender and process as finely as possible. With the motor running, slowly add the oil through the feeder tube in a thin stream to give a smooth paste. Add the cheese and pulse quickly 3–4 times.

Adjust the seasoning if necessary, then scrape the pesto into a small pan and heat gently.

Bring a saucepan of lightly salted water to the boil. Add the tagliatelle and cook for the time stated on the packet. Drain and serve in individual bowls, topping each portion with 2–3 spoonfuls of pesto. Garnish each serving with basil sprigs.

COOK'S TIP

Pesto also makes an excellent dressing for small new potatoes. Serve while still hot or allow to cool to room temperature.

NOODLES WITH CHERRY TOMATOES AND BASIL

Baking the cherry tomatoes slowly with plenty of fresh basil strengthens the taste of this summery dish.

Serves 4–6

1kg/2¼lb cherry tomatoes

3 garlic cloves, finely sliced

1 bunch of basil

120ml/4fl oz/½ cup extra virgin olive oil, plus extra for serving

450g/1lb somen noodles

salt and ground black pepper

shavings of Parmesan cheese and tiny basil sprigs, to garnish

COOK'S TIP

If you can find yellow tomatoes, use half and half to make this dish extra special.

Preheat the oven to 180°C/350°F/Gas 4. Cut the tomatoes in half and arrange, cut-side up, in a single layer in a baking dish. Season with salt and pepper and sprinkle with the sliced garlic. Strip the basil leaves from the stems, then arrange half over the tomatoes. Drizzle the olive oil over the top. Bake the tomatoes for about 1–1½ hours, then set aside in a cool place until ready to serve.

Bring a saucepan of lightly salted water to the boil. Add the noodles and cook for the time stated on the packet. Drain well, tip into a bowl and toss lightly with the baked tomatoes and their juices.

Add the remaining basil, with more olive oil and plenty of salt and pepper. Serve at once, garnished with Parmesan shavings and a few basil sprigs.

BAKED TORTELLINI WITH BASIL

Serve this straight out of the oven while the cheese is still runny and the aroma of the basil is at its peak.

Serves 4–6

450g/1lb/4 cups fresh tortellini

350g/12oz/1½ cups ricotta or full fat
  soft cheese

2 eggs

25g/1oz/2 tbsp butter

25g/1oz/1 cup fresh basil leaves

115g/4oz smoked mozzarella cheese,
  grated

60ml/4 tbsp freshly grated
  Parmesan cheese

salt and ground black pepper

VARIATION

*If smoked mozzarella cheese is
not available, try using a
smoked German cheese or even
grated smoked Cheddar.*

Preheat the oven to 190°C/375°F/Gas 5. Bring a saucepan of lightly salted water to the boil. Add the tortellini and cook for the time stated on the packet. Drain well.

Beat the ricotta until creamy. Beat in the eggs and season well with salt and pepper. Use the butter to grease an ovenproof dish. Spoon in half the tortellini, pour over half the ricotta mixture and cover with half the basil leaves.

Cover with the smoked cheese and remaining basil. Top with the rest of the tortellini and spread over the remaining ricotta mixture. Sprinkle with Parmesan and bake for 35–45 minutes, or until golden brown and bubbling.

MEDITERRANEAN SALAD WITH BASIL

Basil accentuates the Mediterranean flavours in this variation on Salade Niçoise.

Serves 4

225g/8oz/2 cups chunky
*   pasta shapes*
175g/6oz fine green beans, trimmed
2 large ripe tomatoes
50g/2oz/2 cups fresh basil leaves
200g/7oz can tuna in oil, drained
*   and roughly flaked*
2 hard-boiled eggs, shelled and sliced
*   or quartered*
50g/2oz can anchovy fillets, drained
capers
black olives, stoned

For the dressing

90ml/6 tbsp extra virgin olive oil
30ml/2 tbsp white wine vinegar or
*   lemon juice*
2 garlic cloves, crushed
2.5ml/½ tsp Dijon mustard
30ml/2 tbsp chopped fresh basil
salt and ground black pepper

Whisk all the ingredients for the dressing in a bowl and leave to infuse while you make the salad.

Bring a saucepan of lightly salted water to the boil. Add the pasta and cook for the time stated on the packet. Drain well and tip into a bowl. Toss with a little of the dressing and set aside.

Blanch the beans in a pan of boiling lightly salted water for 3 minutes. Drain, refresh under cold water. Drain again.

Slice or quarter the tomatoes and arrange on the bottom of a bowl. Moisten with a little dressing and cover with a quarter of the basil leaves. Top with the beans. Moisten with a little more dressing and cover with a third of the remaining basil.

Cover with the lightly dressed pasta shapes, half the remaining basil and the flaked tuna.

Arrange the eggs on top, then finally scatter over the anchovy fillets, capers and black olives. Pour over the remaining dressing and garnish with the remaining basil. Serve immediately.

PRAWNS AND THAI BASIL

Thai or Grapao basil can be found in most oriental food markets.

Serves 4–6

45ml/3 tbsp vegetable oil

1 egg, beaten

1 onion, chopped

15ml/1 tbsp chopped garlic

15ml/1 tbsp shrimp paste

450g/1lb/2 cups jasmine rice, cooked

350g/12oz cooked prawns, peeled
and deveined

50g/2oz/ ½ cup frozen peas, thawed

oyster sauce, to taste

2 spring onions, chopped

15–20 fresh Thai basil leaves,
roughly torn, plus an extra sprig
to garnish

COOK'S TIP

Cook the rice according to the
directions on the packet.
Although leftover rice can be
used for this recipe, freshly
cooked rice works better.

Heat 15ml/1 tbsp of the oil in a wok. Add the beaten egg and swirl it around to set like a thin pancake. Cook until golden, then slide out on to a board, roll up and cut into thin strips. Set aside.

Heat the remaining oil in the wok, add the onion and garlic and stir-fry for 2–3 minutes. Stir in the shrimp paste and mix well. Add the rice, prawns and peas and toss over the heat until everything is hot.

Season with oyster sauce to taste, taking great care as the shrimp paste is salty. Add the spring onions and basil leaves. Transfer to a serving dish and serve topped with the strips of egg pancake. Garnish with a basil sprig.

TOMATO RISOTTO WITH BASIL

Use plum tomatoes in this dish. Their fresh vibrant flavour is the perfect foil for the basil.

Serves 4

675g/1½lb firm ripe tomatoes,
preferably plum tomatoes
50g/2oz/4 tbsp butter
1 onion, finely chopped
about 1.2 litres/2 pints/5 cups
vegetable stock
275g/10oz/1½ cups arborio rice
400g/14oz can cannellini
beans, drained
50g/2oz/⅔ cup grated Parmesan
cheese, plus extra to garnish
salt and ground black pepper
10–12 fresh basil leaves, to garnish

COOK'S TIP

Shave the Parmesan by using
a swivel-bladed potato peeler.

Cut the tomatoes in half and scoop out the seeds into a sieve placed over a bowl. Press the seeds with a spoon to extract all the juice. Set aside. Grill the tomatoes skin-side up until the skins are blackened. Rub off the skins and dice the flesh.

Melt the butter in a large pan, add the onion and cook for 5 minutes. Add the tomatoes with the reserved juice. Season, then cook for 10 minutes.

Meanwhile, bring the vegetable stock to the boil in another pan.

Add the rice to the tomato mixture and stir to coat. Add a ladleful of the stock and stir gently until absorbed. Repeat, adding a ladleful of stock at a time, until all the stock is absorbed and the rice is tender and creamy. Stir in the beans and Parmesan and heat through for a few minutes. Serve, sprinkling each portion with shredded basil leaves and grated Parmesan.

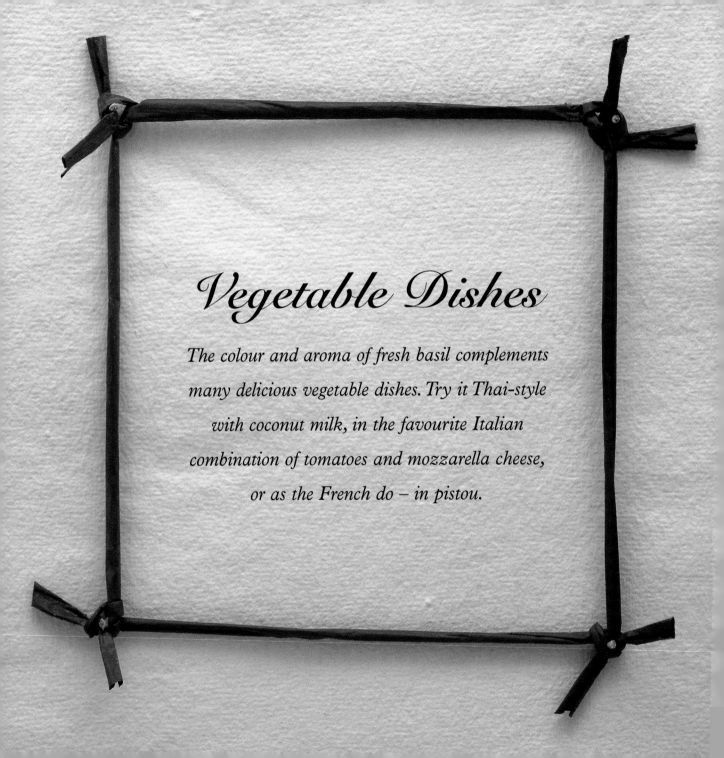

Vegetable Dishes

The colour and aroma of fresh basil complements many delicious vegetable dishes. Try it Thai-style with coconut milk, in the favourite Italian combination of tomatoes and mozzarella cheese, or as the French do – in pistou.

VEGETABLES IN COCONUT MILK AND BASIL

This delectable way of cooking vegetables comes from Thailand. Adding the basil at the last minute produces a mouth-watering aroma.

Serves 4–6

*450g/1lb mixed vegetables, such as
  aubergines, baby sweetcorn,
  carrots, fine green beans, patty
  pan squash*
*8 fresh red chillies, seeded and
  roughly chopped*
2 lemon grass stalks, chopped
4 kaffir lime leaves, torn
30ml/2 tbsp vegetable oil
250ml/8fl oz/1 cup coconut milk
30ml/2 tbsp fish sauce
salt
15–20 Thai basil leaves, to garnish

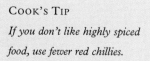
COOK'S TIP
*If you don't like highly spiced
food, use fewer red chillies.*

Cut the mixed vegetables into even shapes of similar size. Put the red chillies, lemon grass and kaffir lime leaves in a mortar and grind to a paste with a pestle.

Heat the oil in a wok. Add the chilli paste and fry for 2–3 minutes, then stir in the coconut milk and bring to the boil. Add the vegetables and cook for about 5 minutes, or until they are tender. Season with the fish sauce and salt and garnish with basil leaves.

AUBERGINE AND BASIL PARCELS

These are delicious little Italian bundles of tomatoes, mozzarella cheese and basil leaves, all wrapped up in generous slices of aubergine, served with a tomato dressing and nutty garnish.

Serves 4

2 large long aubergines

225g/8oz mozzarella cheese

2 plum tomatoes

16 large fresh basil leaves

30ml/2 tbsp olive oil

salt and ground black pepper

toasted pine nuts and torn basil
   leaves, to garnish

For the tomato dressing

60ml/4 tbsp olive oil

5ml/1 tsp balsamic vinegar

15ml/1 tbsp sun-dried tomato paste

15ml/1 tbsp lemon juice

Remove the stalks from the aubergines and cut the aubergines lengthways into thin slices. Bring a large saucepan of lightly salted water to the boil and cook the aubergine slices for about 2 minutes, until just softened. Drain, then dry on kitchen paper.

Cut the mozzarella cheese into eight slices. Cut each tomato into eight slices, not counting the first and last slices.

Take two aubergine slices and arrange one on top of the other in the form of a cross. Place a slice of tomato in the centre, season with salt and pepper, then add a basil leaf, followed by a slice of mozzarella, another basil leaf, a slice of tomato and more seasoning. Fold the ends of the aubergine slices around the mozzarella and tomato filling to make a neat parcel. Repeat with the rest of the assembled ingredients to make eight parcels. Place the parcels on a baking sheet and chill for about 20 minutes.

Make the tomato dressing. Whisk the olive oil, vinegar, sun-dried tomato paste and lemon juice in a bowl. Season to taste.

Preheat the grill. Brush the parcels with olive oil and grill for 5 minutes on each side until golden. Serve hot, with the dressing, sprinkled with pine nuts and basil leaves.

MARINATED VEGETABLES WITH BASIL OIL

Basil oil is a must for drizzling over plain stir-fried vegetables. Once it has been made up, it will keep in the fridge for up to 2 weeks.

Serves 2–4

15ml/1 tbsp olive oil

1 garlic clove, crushed

finely grated rind of 1 lemon

400g/14oz can artichoke hearts, drained

2 large leeks, sliced

225g/8oz patty pan squash, halved if large

115g/4oz plum tomatoes, cut into segments lengthways

15g/½oz/½ cup basil leaves

150ml/¼ pint/⅔ cup extra virgin olive oil

VARIATION

Use courgettes, cut into batons, instead of patty pan squash, and whole cherry tomatoes in place of plum tomatoes.

Mix the olive oil, garlic and lemon rind in a bowl, to make a marinade. Place the artichokes, leeks, patty pan squash and plum tomatoes in a large bowl, pour over the marinade and leave for 30 minutes.

Meanwhile, make the basil oil. Purée the basil leaves with the olive oil in a food processor or blender, then scrape into a jug.

Heat a wok, add the marinated vegetables and stir-fry for 3–4 minutes, tossing well. Drizzle the basil oil over the vegetables and serve.

VEGETABLE AND BASIL KEBABS

Vegetables nestling in basil and mint leaves make great kebabs – choose any vegetables in season.

Serves 4

24 mushrooms

16 cherry tomatoes

16 thick slices of courgette

16 squares of red pepper

16 basil leaves, plus extra to garnish

16 large mint leaves

To baste

115g/4oz/½ cup butter, melted

1 garlic clove, crushed

15ml/1 tbsp crushed
  green peppercorns

salt

For the sauce

50g/2oz/¼ cup butter

45ml/3 tbsp brandy

250ml/8fl oz/1 cup double cream

5ml/1 tsp crushed green peppercorns

Thread the vegetables on to eight skewers, placing the basil leaves next to the tomatoes, and wrapping the mint leaves around the courgette slices. Preheat the grill or prepare the barbecue.

Mix the basting ingredients and baste the kebabs thoroughly. Place the skewers under the grill or on a grid over medium-hot coals, turning and basting regularly for about 5–7 minutes until the vegetables are just cooked.

Heat the butter for the sauce in a frying pan, then add the brandy and light it. When the flames have died down, stir in the cream and the peppercorns. Cook for about 2 minutes, stirring all the time. Serve the kebabs with the green peppercorn sauce, garnished with basil.

COURGETTE FRITTERS WITH PISTOU

These delicious fritters are a speciality of Southern France. The basil pistou provides a contrast in flavour.

Serves 4

450g/1lb courgettes, grated

75g/3oz/ ¾ cup plain flour

1 egg, separated

15ml/1 tbsp olive oil

oil, for shallow frying

salt and ground black pepper

For the pistou

15g/½oz/½ cup basil leaves

4 garlic cloves, crushed

75g/3oz/1 cup grated
   Parmesan cheese

finely grated rind of 1 lemon

150ml/¼ pint/⅔ cup olive oil

Make the pistou. Mix the basil leaves and garlic in a mortar. Crush with a pestle to a fairly fine paste. Transfer the paste to a bowl and stir in the grated cheese and lemon rind. Whisk in the oil, a little at a time, to make a sauce, then transfer to a small serving dish.

Put the grated courgettes in a sieve over a mixing bowl and sprinkle with plenty of salt. Leave for 1 hour, then rinse thoroughly. Drain and dry well on kitchen paper.

Sift the flour into a bowl and make a well in the centre, then add the egg yolk and oil. Measure 75ml/5 tbsp water and add a little to the bowl. Whisk the egg yolk and oil, gradually incorporating the flour and remaining water to make a smooth batter. Season and leave for 30 minutes.

Stir the courgettes into the batter. Whisk the egg white until stiff, then fold it into the batter.

Heat 1cm/½in of oil in a frying pan. Add generous spoonfuls of batter to the oil and fry in batches for 2 minutes until golden. Drain the courgette fritters on kitchen paper and keep hot while frying the rest. Serve with the pistou.

COOK'S TIP

Don't overcrowd the pan when cooking the fritters, or you may find it difficult to lift them out.

INDEX

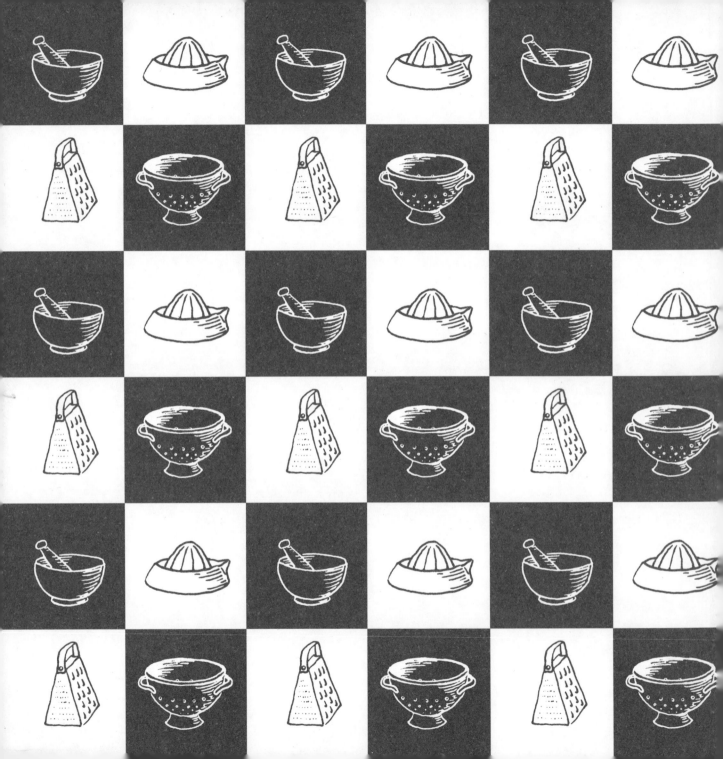